The Body

Heart

Veronica Ross

Chrysalis Children's Books

First published in the UK in 2004 by
(✦) Chrysalis Children's Books,
An imprint of Chrysalis Books Group PLC
The Chrysalis Building, Bramley Road, London W10 6SP

ISBN 1 84458 092 X

British Library Cataloguing in Publication Data
for this book is available from the British Library.

Editorial manager: Joyce Bentley
Editors: Rosalind Beckman, Joe Fullman
Illustrator: Chris Forsey
Designer: Wladek Szechter
Picture researcher: Jenny Barlow

Printed in China

10 9 8 7 6 5 4 3 2 1

Words in **bold** can be found in Words to remember on page 30.

Picture credits
Angela Hampton/Family Life Picture Library: FC, 4, 8, 15, 26.
Corbis: FC (Inset), 5; Tim Pannell 9.
Digital Vision: 22, 23.
Getty Images: Catherine Ledner 1, 7; Bob Thomas 16.
Rex: Ted Blackbrow FC (Inset), 27; International Magazine Service FC (Inset), 25; Nils
Jorgensen 21.
Science Photo Library: Mark Clarke FC (Inset), 13; D. Phillips 12; Science Photo Library 14;
Dr P Marazzi 17; Pascal Goetgheluck 18; Stevie Grand 20; CC Studio 28.
Stockbyte: 24.
Wellcome Photo Library: Anthea Sieveking 11.
Illustrations: Chris Forsey 6, 8, 10, 18,9, 29, back cover (inset).

Contents

Look at me!

I can jump and play and do my exercises.

My **heart** is the most important part in my body.

It **beats** all the time and that keeps me alive.

Exercise helps to keep your heart strong and healthy.

Your heart started working before you were born and it will carry on working every day of your life.

You heart beats when you sleep, eat, walk, talk, play – and ice skate!

Where is my heart?

Your heart is inside your chest. It is about the same size as your fist and the same shape as a pear. Your heart grows bigger as you grow bigger.

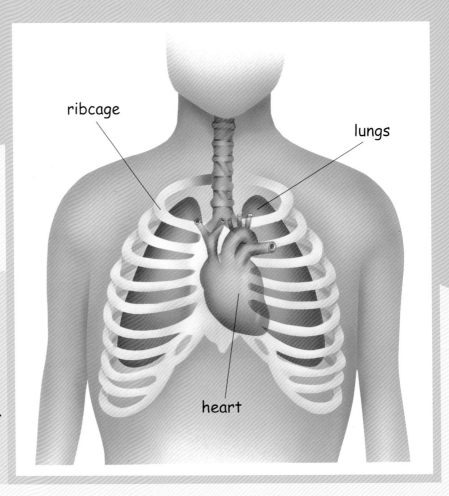

ribcage

lungs

heart

The **bones** in your chest that make up your **ribcage** protect your heart.

An adult's heart is the same size
as his or her fist.

Your heart is between your
lungs, on the left side of your chest.
Put you hand on your chest and see if
you can feel your heart beating.

A healthy heart can beat over
two billion times in a lifetime.

What is my heart?

Your heart is a **muscle**. You have lots of
muscles all over your body, but your heart
is a very special muscle because it sends
blood to all parts of your body.

Your heart works all day and all night and never
gets tired. It is the busiest part of your body.

Your heart takes about 20 seconds to pump blood to every part of your body.

Your body needs a steady supply of blood to keep working properly so that you can run and play.

How does my heart work?

Your heart is a like a bag with walls made of strong muscle. Before each beat, your heart fills with blood.

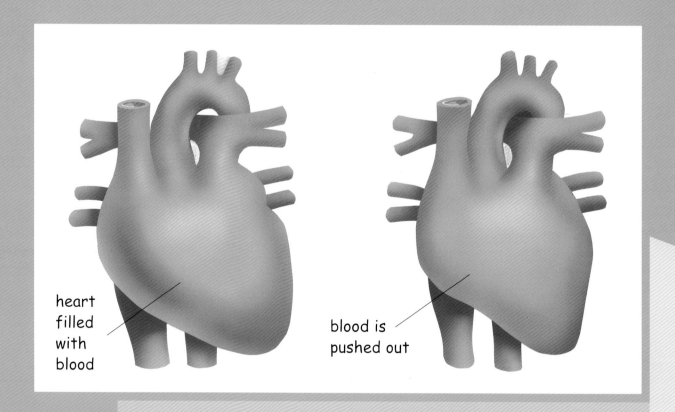

heart
filled
with
blood

blood is
pushed out

Your heart changes shape as it beats. It relaxes, or loosens up, to let the blood flow in. Then it tightens to push the blood out.

Then the muscles tighten to pump the blood out and around your body. Your **heartbeat** is the sound of your blood being pumped in and out of your heart.

You may be able to hear your friend's heart beating if you listen hard to his chest.

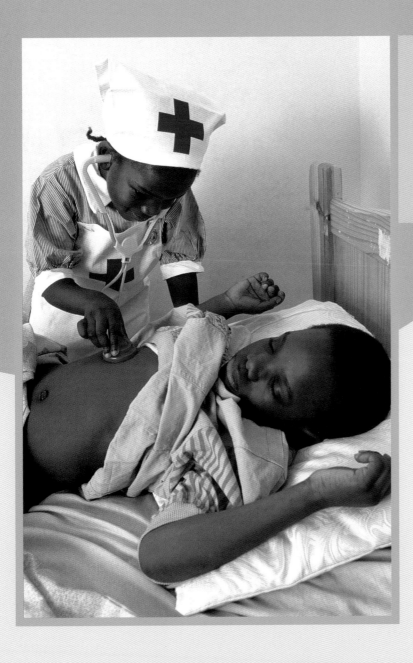

Your blood

Blood is the red liquid that carries a gas called **oxygen** all around your body. Your body takes in oxygen when you breathe.

Red blood **cells** in your blood carry oxygen to all the parts of your body.

Your body uses the oxygen to make **energy**. You need energy to do all the things you like to do.

You can see your blood if you fall and cut yourself.

Your body contains about three litres of blood – that's about the same as three large cartons of orange juice.

Fighting germs

In your blood, there are also white blood cells. They attack **germs** that get into your body.

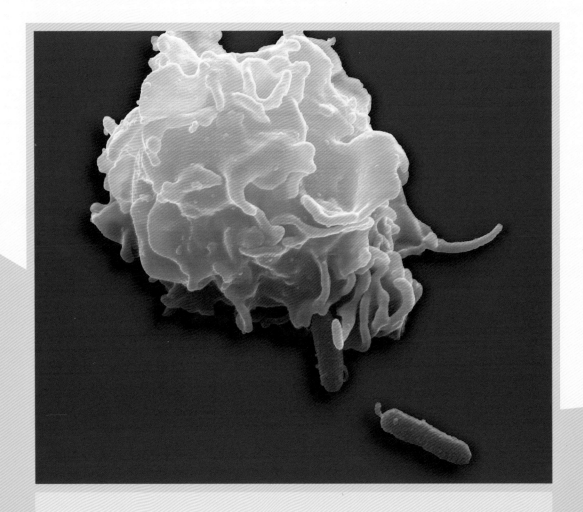

White blood cells hunt down germs and destroy them. The white blood cell is at the top of the picture. The germs are in red at the bottom.

Most germs are harmless, but some can cause **diseases** that make you ill.

Your doctor can help to protect you against some diseases by giving you an **injection**.

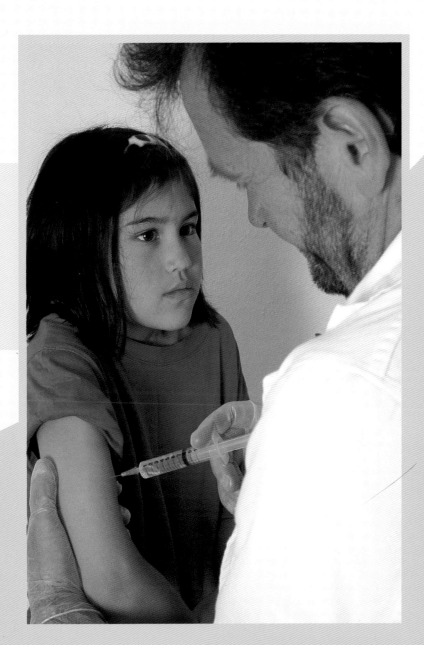

Cuts and scabs

When you fall and cut yourself, special parts in your blood stick together to form a clot.

Washing a cut or graze with water cleans it and helps to keep out germs.

The clot stops more blood flowing out of the cut. As the clot dries out, it hardens and makes a scab. This keeps germs out of your body.

Under the scab, the skins heals. The scab will fall off when a new layer of skin has been made.

Blood vessels

Your heart is attached to soft, bendy tubes called blood vessels.

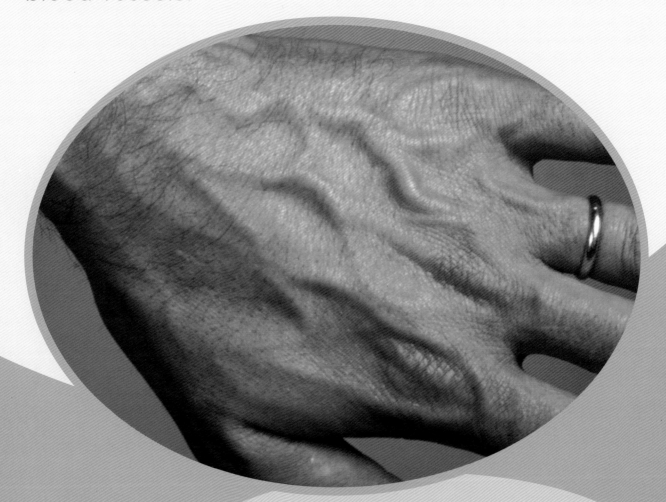

Look at the back of a grown-up's hand and you might be able to see blue lines. These are blood vessels called veins.

The blood vessels take the blood to every part of your body, from the top of your head to your fingers and toes.

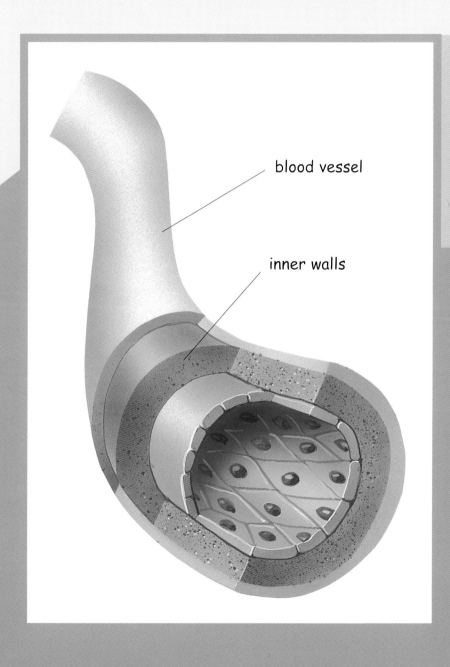

blood vessel

inner walls

The blood vessels that carry the blood away from your heart are wide and thick.

Noisy heart

A doctor uses a **stethoscope** to listen carefully to your heart to make sure it is working properly.

Your heart makes a lub-dub, lub-dub sound with each beat.

A stethoscope makes the sound
of your heartbeat much louder.

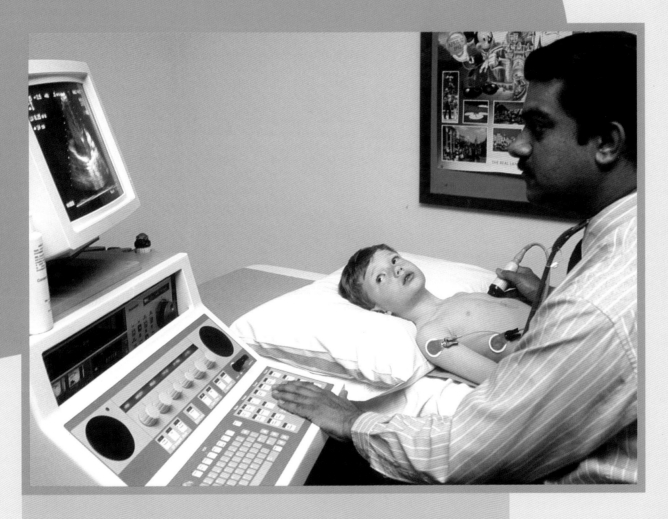

Doctors use an **ultrasound machine** to watch
the heart and the blood flowing though it.

Fast and slow

When you exercise, you breathe more quickly to take in more air. This makes your heart pump faster to carry the extra oxygen you need all around your body.

Your heart rate is slowest when you are fast asleep.

If you exercise really hard, your heart can beat twice as fast as normal.

Your heart beats about 80-100 times a minute.

Look after your heart

Fatty, sugary foods, such as crisps, cakes and biscuits aren't good for your heart, so try not to eat too many of them.

Fizzy drinks have lots of sugar. A glass of milk or juice is much better for you.

Rice, bread, potatoes and pasta
fill you up and give you energy.

Try to
eat some fruit
and vegetables
every day.

Exercise is fun

You need to take care of your heart if you want to keep it working properly.

Running, cycling, swimming and gymnastics will all help to keep your heart in good shape.

Exercise is a great way to keep your heart muscles healthy. The more you use your heart, the stronger it will be.

Cycling is a good way to stay fit, but make sure you wear a helmet to **protect** your head.

Taking a pulse

Each time your heart beats, it tightens to pump blood around the body. This can be felt as a **pulse**.

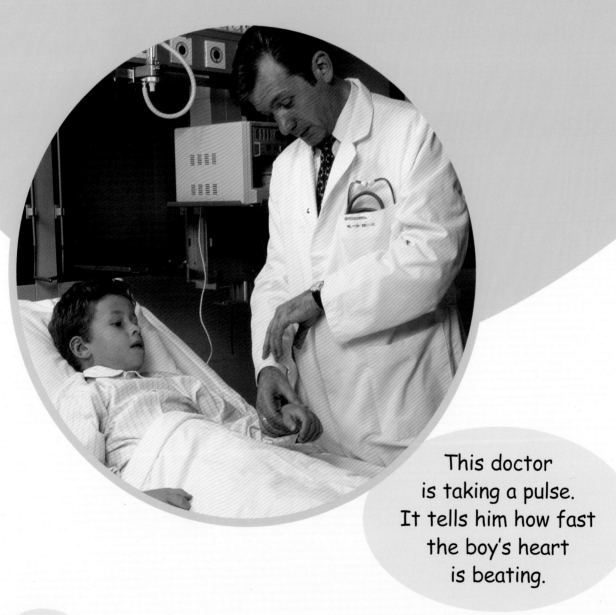

This doctor is taking a pulse. It tells him how fast the boy's heart is beating.

You can feel your pulse in your neck,
the back of your knee, your elbow
and your wrist.

Place two fingertips on your wrist just below
your thumb. Can you feel a beat under the skin?
This is your pulse.

Words to remember

beat To pump. When your heart beats, it pumps blood around your body.

blood The red liquid full of oxygen that is pumped around your body by your heart.

bones The hard and tough parts inside your body that make up your skeleton.

cells The tiny living parts that make up your body. There are many different types of cells.

disease An illness.

energy The power you need to be able to work and play.

germs Tiny things that are all around us. Some germs can make you ill.

heart The muscle that pumps blood around your body.

heartbeat The sound your heart makes as it pumps blood around your body.

injection Medicine given to a person to help protect against diseases.

lungs The soft, spongy parts inside your chest that allow you to breathe.

muscle The soft, stretchy parts inside your body that make you move.

oxygen A gas found in the air that you need in order to breathe.

protect To look after.

pulse The beat that can be felt in your neck, knee, elbow and wrist. It is made by blood being pumped around your body by your heart.

ribcage The bones in your chest that protect your heart and lungs.

stethoscope An instrument for listening to the sounds made inside your body.

ultrasound machine A machine used to see inside the body.

Index